Everybody's Favorite Series No. 69

Trade Mark

19 Market Street
Tavistock, Devon
PL19 0DE
Telephone (0822) 614074

Wedding and Sacred Music for Organ

With Lyrics and Registrations for All Organs

FOREWORD *Everybody's Favorite Wedding and Sacred Music combines in one volume a collection of perennially popular sacred and wedding numbers. The arrangements are fairly easy and can be readily played by most organists without difficulty. The registration is for pipe organs of all dimensions and for the Hammond. It can also be applied to other electric organs as these registrations are mere suggestions rather than fast rules.*

Concerning the selections for Weddings, the music chosen is varied enough to present suitable material for before and during the service. These pieces are presented in the order in which they would be played if all of them were used. Such numbers as "Wedding Prelude" or "On Wings of Song" may be played very softly as background music during the service. The other selections are suitable for church service, for studio or home use as well.

Dr. Diggle has been active in performing, composing and teaching for many years. Some of his original works are included here. **THE PUBLISHER**

Copyright © 1948 (Renewed) by Amsco Music Publishing Company,
A Division of Music Sales Corporation, New York
All Right Reserved

Order No. AM40288
International Standard Book Number: 0.8256.2069.4

Exclusive Distributors:
Music Sales Corporation
225 Park Avenue South, New York, NY
Music Sales Limited
8/9 Frith Street, London W1V 5TZ England
Music Sales Pty. Limited
120 Rothschild Street, Rosebery, Sydney, NSW 2018, Australia

Printed in the United States of America by
Vicks Lithograph and Printing Corporation

Contents

WEDDING MUSIC

		Page			Page
Angel's Serenade	G. Braga	28	On Wings Of Song	F. Mendelssohn	14
Ave Maria	F. Schubert	6	O Promise Me	R. De Koven	17
Ave Maria	Bach-Gounod	22	Thou Art Like A Flower	R. Schumann	27
Bridal Chorus	R. Wagner	20	Wedding March	F. Mendelssohn	32
Dedication	R. Franz	26	Wedding Prelude	R. Diggle	11
I Love Thee	E. Grieg	4			

CHRISTMAS CAROLS

First Nowell, The	Traditional	153	O Holy Night (Cantique De Noel)	A. Adam	150
It Came Upon The Midnight Clear	R. Willis	152	Silent Night, Holy Night	F. Gruber	156
O Come All Ye Faithful	J. Reading	154	Star Of The East	A. Kennedy	148

SACRED MUSIC FOR OTHER OCCASIONS

Adore And Be Still	C. Gounod	38	Luther's Cradle Hymn	Luther-Vibbard	145
Agnus Dei	G. Bizet	101	Mine Eyes Have Seen The Glory	Howe-Steffe	143
Ave Verum	W. Mozart	40	My Faith Looks Up To Thee (Reverie)	R. Diggle	90
But The Lord Is Mindful	F. Mendelssohn	41	Nazareth	C. Gounod	124
Christians Awake	J. Wainright	136	Not A Sparrow Falleth	F. Abt	116
Come Sweet Peace	J. S. Bach	138	O Divine Redeemer	C. Gounod	65
Communion Hymn	17th Century Melody Arr. by R. Diggle	134	Onward Christian Soldiers	A. Sullivan	142
Cross Of Calvary, The	C. Gounod	120	Open The Gates Of The Temple	J. F. Knapp	140
Cujus Animan	G. Rossini	96	O Rest In The Lord	F. Mendelssohn	70
Eye Hath Not Seen	A. R. Gaul	112	Panis Angelicus	C. Franck	104
Hark, Hark My Soul	H. R. Shelley	128	Pilgrim's Song	P. Tschaikowsky	72
Hear My Prayer (Prelude)	F. Mendelssohn	51	Rocked In The Cradle Of The Deep	J. P. Knight	144
He Shall Feed His Flock	G. Handel	43	Safe In The Arms Of Jesus (Meditation)	R. Diggle	146
If With All Your Hearts	F. Mendelssohn	46	Sun Of My Soul	P. Ritter	132
I Know That My Redeemer Liveth	G. Handel	48	Take My Hand, Precious Lord	T. Dorsey	111
I'm A Pilgrim	H. Johnson	126	Then Shall The Righteous Shine Forth	F. Mendelssohn	80
I Waited For The Lord	F. Mendelssohn	54	There Is A Green Hill	C. Gounod	82
I Walked Into The Garden	M. Weaver	139	These Are They Which Came	A. R. Gaul	86
I Will Extol Thee, O Lord	M. Costa	75	Were You There When They Crucified My Lord	Spiritual	122
Jesu, Joy Of Man's Desiring	J. S. Bach	57			
King Of Love, The	C. Gounod	60			
Largo (From Xerxes)	G. Handel	63			
List, The Cherubic Host	A. R. Gaul	92			
Litany For The Feast Of All Saints	F. Schubert	107			
Lost Chord, The	A. Sullivan	108			

Registrations for All Organs appear on Page 157.

COMPOSER INDEX

ABT, F.
Not A Sparrow Falleth 116

ADAM, A.
O Holy Night (Cantique de Noel) 150

BACH, J. S.
Come Sweet Peace 138
Jesu, Joy of Man's Desiring 57

BACH-GOUNOD
Ave Maria 22

BIZET, G.
Agnus Dei 101

BRAGA, G.
Angel's Serenade 28

COSTA, M.
I Will Extol Thee, O Lord 75

DE KOVEN, R.
O Promise Me 17

DIGGLE, R.
Communion Hymn (17th Century Melody) ... 134
My Faith Looks Up To Thee
Safe In The Arms Of Jesus (Meditation) ... 146
Wedding Prelude (Salut D'Amour)

DORSEY, T.
Take My Hand, Precious Lord 111

FRANCK, C.
Panis Angelicus 104

FRANZ, R.
Dedication 26

GAUL, A. R.
Eye Hath Not Seen 112
List, The Cherubic Host 92
These Are They Which Came 86

GOUNOD, C.
Adore And Be Still 38
Cross Of Cavalry, The 120
King Of Love, The 60
Nazareth 124
O Divine Redeemer 65
There Is A Green Hill 82

GRIEG, E.
I Love Thee 4

GRUBER, F.
Silent Night, Holy Night 156

HANDEL, G.
He Shall Feed His Flock 43
I Know That My Redeemer Liveth 48
Largo (From Xerxes) 63

HOWE-STEFFE
Mine Eyes Have Seen The Glory 143

JOHNSON, H.
I'm A Pilgrim 126

KENNEDY, A.
Star Of The East 148

KNAPP, J. F.
Open The Gates Of The Temple 140

KNIGHT, J. P.
Rocked In The Cradle Of The Deep 144

LUTHER-VIBBARD
Luther's Cradle Hymn 145

MENDELSSOHN, F.
But The Lord Is Mindful 41
Hear My Prayer (Prelude) 51
If With All Your Hearts 46
I Waited For The Lord 54
On Wings Of Song 14
O Rest In The Lord 70
Then Shall The Righteous Shine Forth ... 80
Wedding March 32

MOZART, W.
Ave Verum 40

READING, J.
O Come All Ye Faithful 154

RITTER, P.
Sun Of My Soul 132

ROSSINI, G.
Cujus Animan 96

SCHUBERT, F.
Ave Maria 6
Litany For The Feast Of All Saints 107

SCHUMANN, R.
Thou Art Like A Flower 27

SHELLEY, H. R.
Hark, Hark My Soul 128

SPIRITUAL
Were You There When They Crucified My Lord. 122

SULLIVAN, A.
Lost Chord, The 108
Onward Christian Soldiers 142

TRADITIONAL
First Nowell, The 153

TSCHAIKOWSKY, P.
Pilgrim's Song 72

WAGNER, R.
Bridal Chorus 20

WAINRIGHT, J.
Christians Awake 136

WEAVER, M.
I Walked Into The Garden 139

WILLIS, R.
It Came Upon The Midnight Clear 152

I Love Thee
Wedding Prelude

Registration 2

EDWARD GRIEG

Copyright MCMXLVIII by Amsco Music Publishing Co. N.Y.C.   Made in U.S.A.

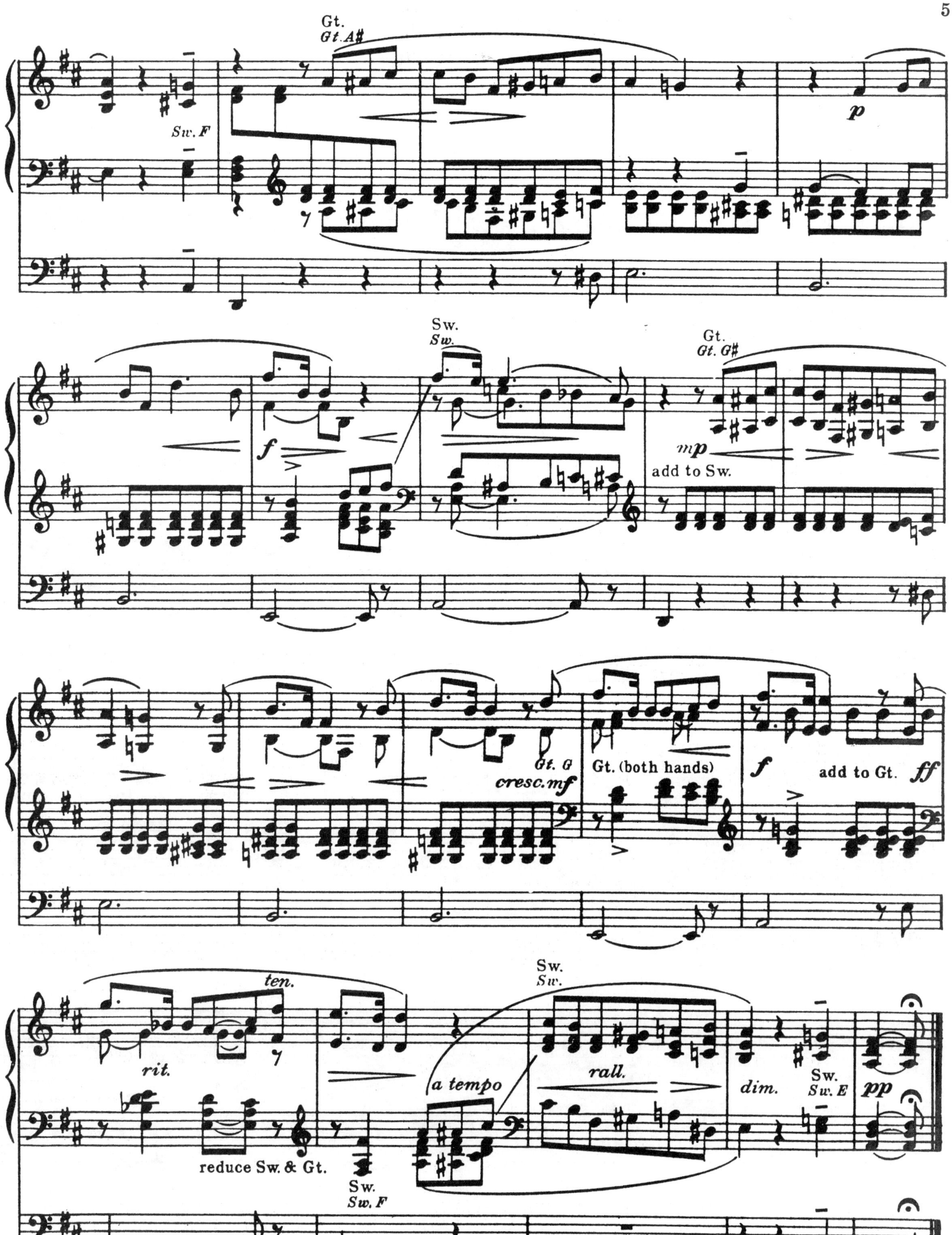
Gt.
Gt. A♯
Sw. F
p
Sw.
Sw.
Gt.
Gt. G♯
f
mp
add to Sw.
Gt. G
cresc. mf
Gt. (both hands)
f
add to Gt.
ff
ten.
rit.
reduce Sw. & Gt.
Sw.
Sw. F
a tempo
Sw.
Sw.
rall.
dim.
Sw.
Sw. E
pp

Ave Maria

Registration 1

SCHUBERT

Copyright MCMXLVIII by Amsco Music Publishing Co. N.Y.C.

Made in U.S.A.

Salut d'Amour
(Wedding Prelude)*

Registration 4

ROLAND DIGGLE

* For music during the service, play with softest stops on Swell and Great without pedal stops but couple Swell to Pedal.

Copyright MCMXLVIII by Amsco Music Publishing Co. N.Y.C.

Made in U.S.A.

On Wings of Song

F. MENDELSSOHN

15

veal ___ The lotus flow-er re-pos-es ___ Her sis-ter's charm to feel. ___ The lo-tus flow-er re-pos ___ es Her sis-ter's charm to feel.

Sw. B

Repeat with change of solo stop ‖2   *Gt. B*

A-bide with me un-der the

rall.

Bridal Chorus
(Lohengrin)

Registration 15

WAGNER

*If the march has to be lengthened, as it so often is, repeat to this point from the 5th measure, and repeat as often as required.

Ave Maria

Registration 1

BACH-GOUNOD

Copyright MCMXLVIII by Amsco Music Publishing Co. N.Y.C.

Made in U.S.A.

Dedication

ROBERT FRANZ

Thou Art Like a Flower

Registration 2

R. SCHUMANN

La Serenata
(Angel's Serenade)

Registration 11

G. BRAGA

Andante con moto

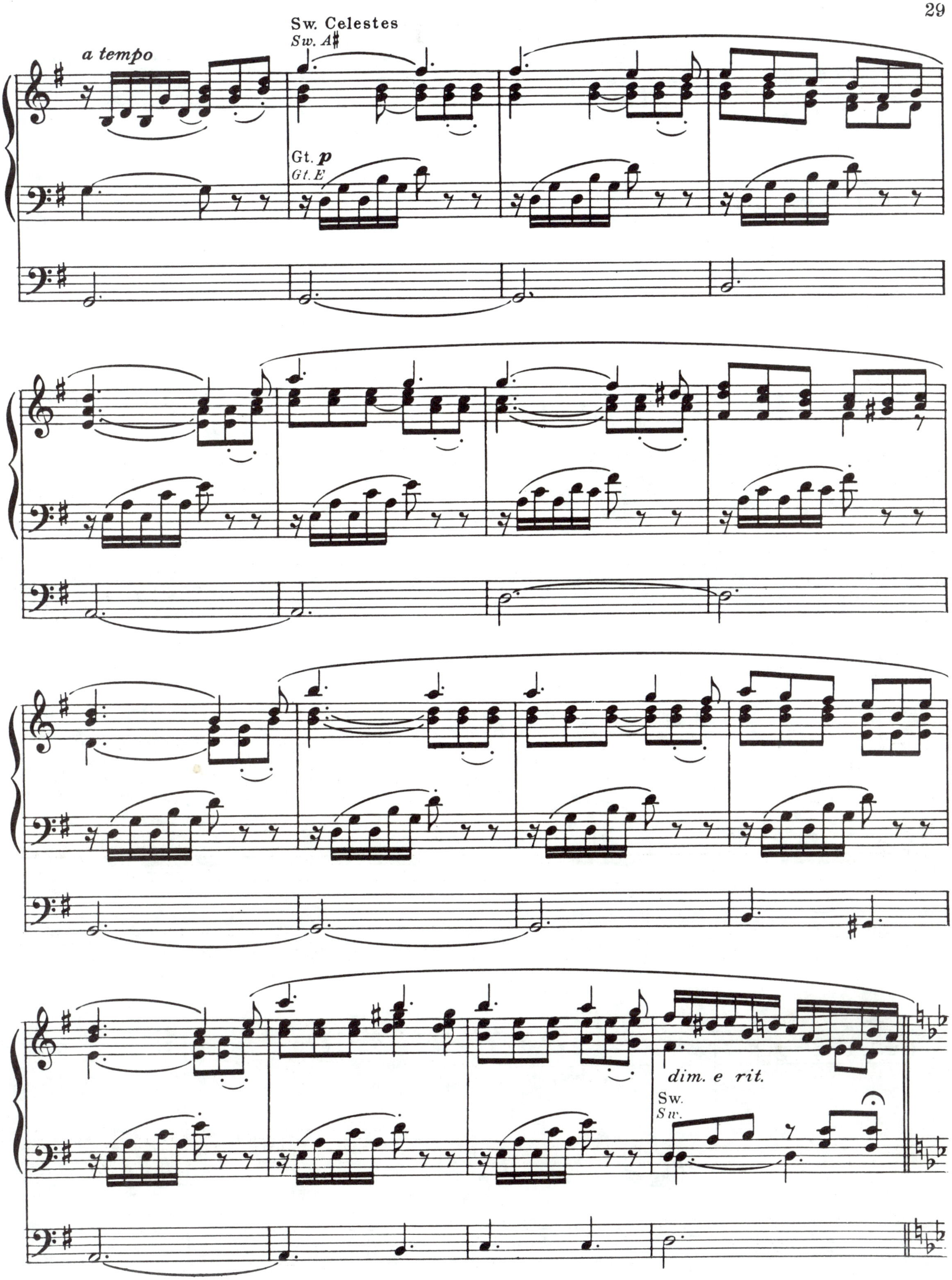
a tempo
Sw. Celestes
Sw. A♯
Gt. p
Gt. E
dim. e rit.
Sw.
Sw.

Wedding March
(Midsummer Night's Dream)

Registration 14

FELIX MENDELSSOHN

* This march may be shortened by omitting the 3rd theme, starting on the 2nd page, and if desired, further abbreviated by omitting the 4th theme, starting on the 4th page.

Copyright MCMXLVIII by Amsco Music Publishing Co. N.Y.C. Made in U.S.A

Ave Verum

Registration 12

W. MOZART

But the Lord is Mindful of His Own
from "ST. PAUL"

Registration 6

F. MENDELSSOHN

Andantino

But the Lord is mind-ful of his own, he re-mem-bers his chil - dren, But the Lord is mind-ful of his own, the Lord re-members his chil-dren, re-mem-bers his chil-dren. Bow down be-fore Him, ye

Copyright MCMXLVIII by Amsco Music Publishing Co. Inc., N.Y.C.

Made in U.S.A.

If with all your hearts
Aria from "Elijah"

Registration 8

MENDELSSOHN

Air
I Know That My Redeemer Liveth

Registration 10

HANDEL

Copyright MCMXLVIII by Amsco Music Publishing Co. N.Y.C.

Made in U.S.A.

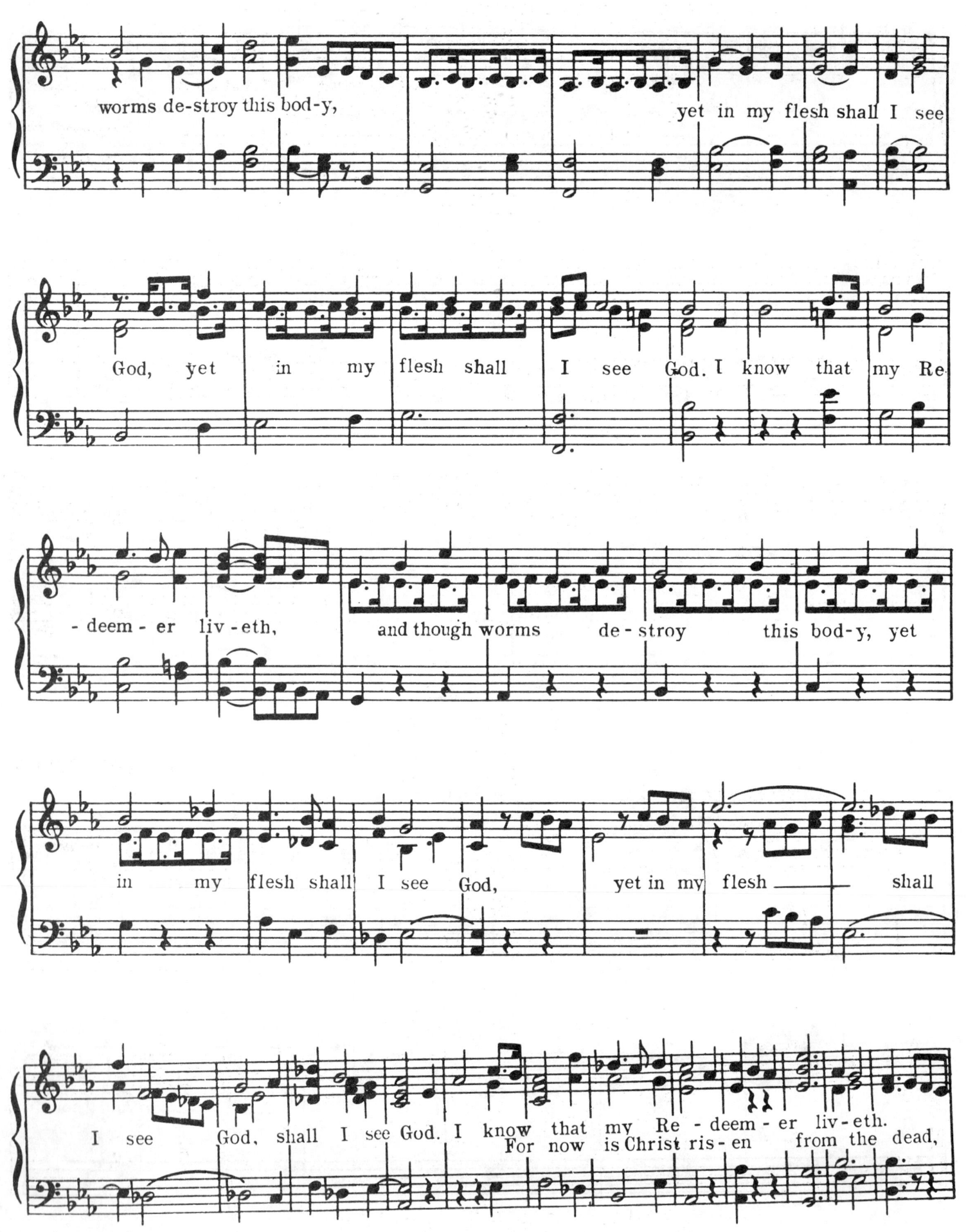

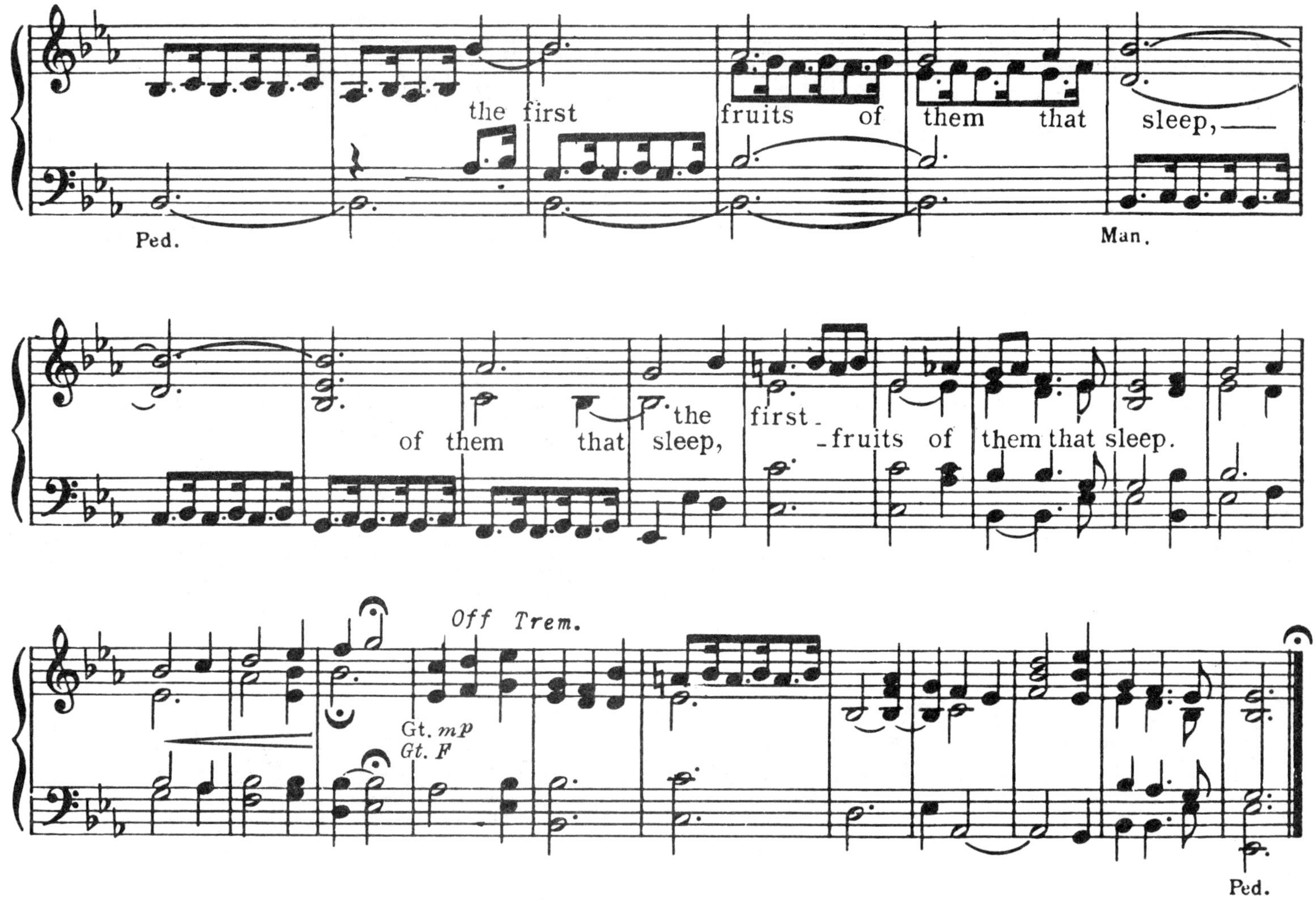

Prelude
Hear My Prayer

Registration 9

MENDELSSOHN

Moderato sostenuto

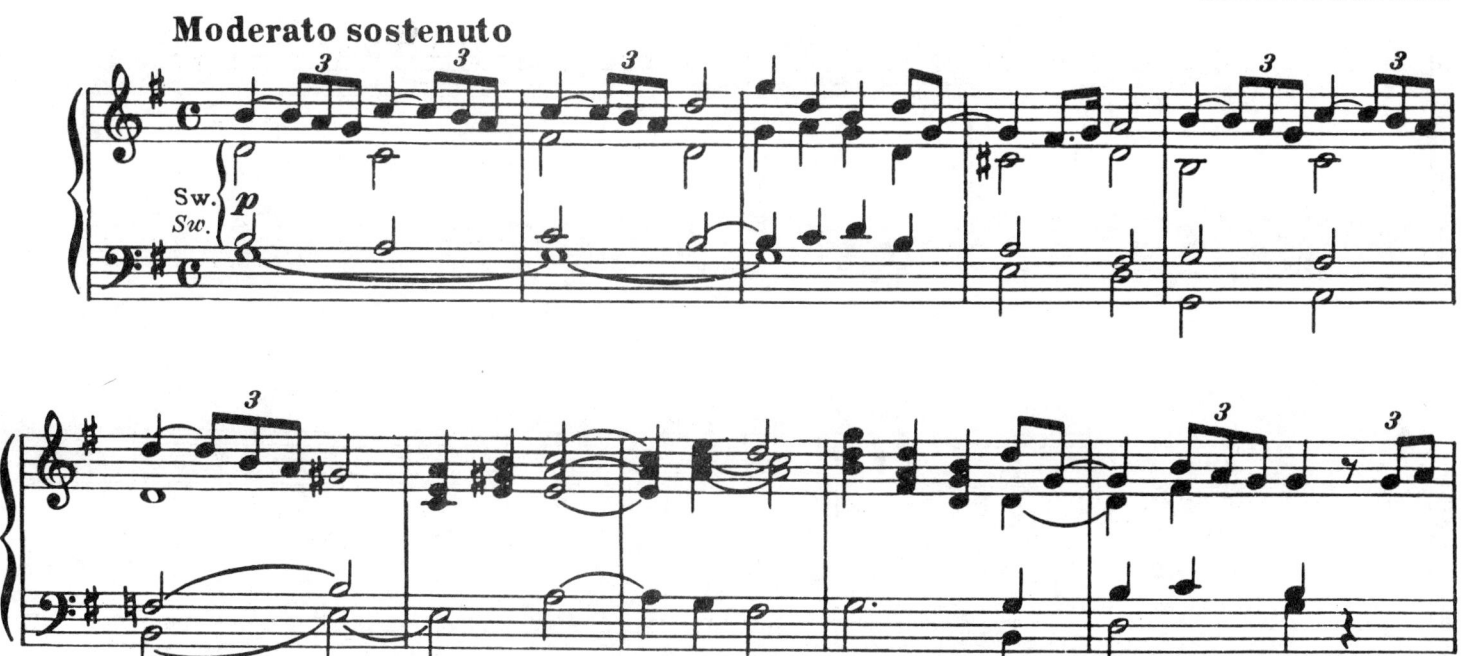

52

I waited for the Lord

Registration 8

F. MENDELSSOHN

Jesu, Joy of Man's Desiring

Registration 7

J. S. BACH

Semplice e grazioso

The King of Love My Shepherd Is

Registration 13

CHARLES GOUNOD

Copyright MCMXLVIII by Amsco Music Publishing Co. N.Y.C.

Made in U.S.A.

Largo in G
(Xerxes)

Registration 6

G. F. HANDEL

64

O Divine Redeemer!

Registration 11

CHARLES GOUNOD

Ah! turn me not a-way___ re-ceive me, tho' un-wor___ thy!

Ah! turn me not a-way,___ re-ceive me, tho' un-wor___ thy! Hear Thou my cry, hear

Copyright MCMXLVIII by Amsco Music Publishing Co. N.Y.C. Made in U.S.A.

69

O Rest in the Lord
From "ELIJAH"

Registration 10

F. MENDELSSOHN

Pilgrim's Song

Registration 12

P. I. TSCHAIKOWSKY

Copyright MCMXLVIII by Amsco Music Publishing Co., N.Y.C.

Made in U.S.A.

I Will Extol Thee, O Lord

Registration 15

M. COSTA

Copyright MCMXLVIII by Amsco Music Publishing Co., N.Y.C.

Made in U.S.A.

78

These Are They Which Came

From "The Holy City"

Registration 4

A. R. GAUL

Copyright MCMXLVIII by Amsco Music Publishing Co. N.Y.C.

Reverie
(My Faith Looks Up to Thee)

Registration 5

ROLAND DIGGLE

Copyright MCMXLVIII by Amsco Music Publishing Co. N.Y.C.

Made in U.S.A.

List! the Cherubic Host

Registration 15

A. R. GAUL

Moderato

List! the cher-u-bic host, in thou-sand choirs,

Copyright MCMXLVIII by Amsco Music Publishing Co., N.Y.C.

Made in U.S.A.

93

Cujus Animam
from "STABAT MATER"

Registration 14

G. A. ROSSINI

Agnus Dei

Registration 3

G. BIZET

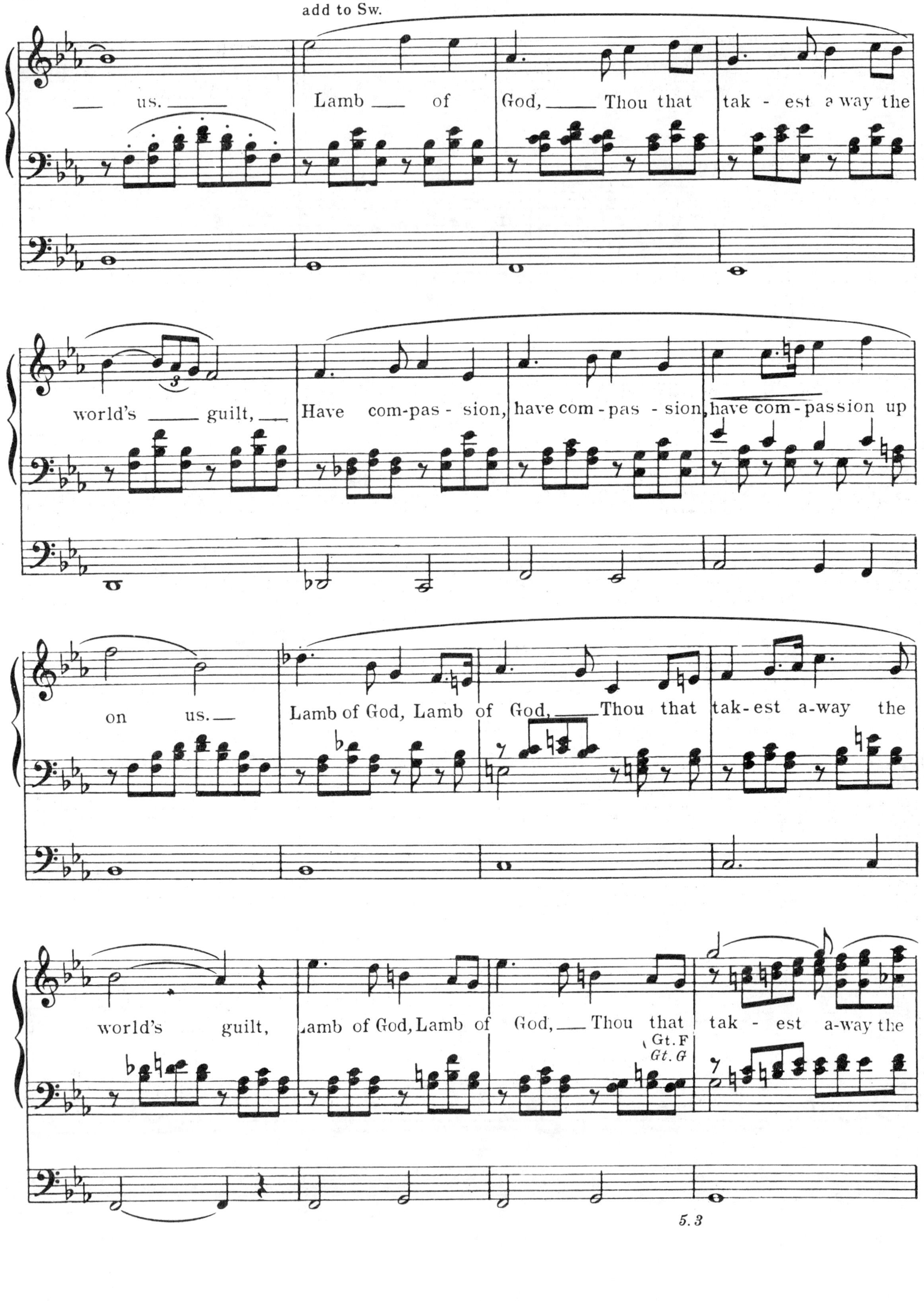
add to Sw.
us. Lamb of God, Thou that tak - est a way the
world's guilt, Have com-pas - sion, have com - pas - sion, have com - passion up
on us. Lamb of God, Lamb of God, Thou that tak-est a-way the
world's guilt, Lamb of God, Lamb of God, Thou that tak - est a-way the
Gt. F
Gt. G
5. 3

Panis Angelicus

Registration 12

CESAR FRANCK

Litany for the Feast of All Saints

Registration 4

F. SCHUBERT

Take My Hand, Precious Lord

Registration 3

THOMAS A. DORSEY

*Used by permission, Thos. A Dorsey, 755 Oakwood Blvd., Chicago, Ill.

Eye Hath Not Seen

Registration 8

A. R. GAUL

Not a Sparrow Falleth

Registration 4

FRANZ ABT

Copyright MCMXLVIII by Amsco Music Publishing Co., N.Y.C.

The Cross of Calvary
(Ave Maria)

CHARLES GOUNOD

Were You There
When They Crucified My Lord

Registration 9

Negro Spiritual

123

Nazareth

Registration 11

GOUNOD

Hark! Hark My Soul

Registration 6

HARRY ROWE SHELLEY

Copyright MCMXLVIII by Amsco Music Publishing Co., N.Y.C.   Made in U.S.A.

Sun of My Soul

Registration 5

P. RITTER

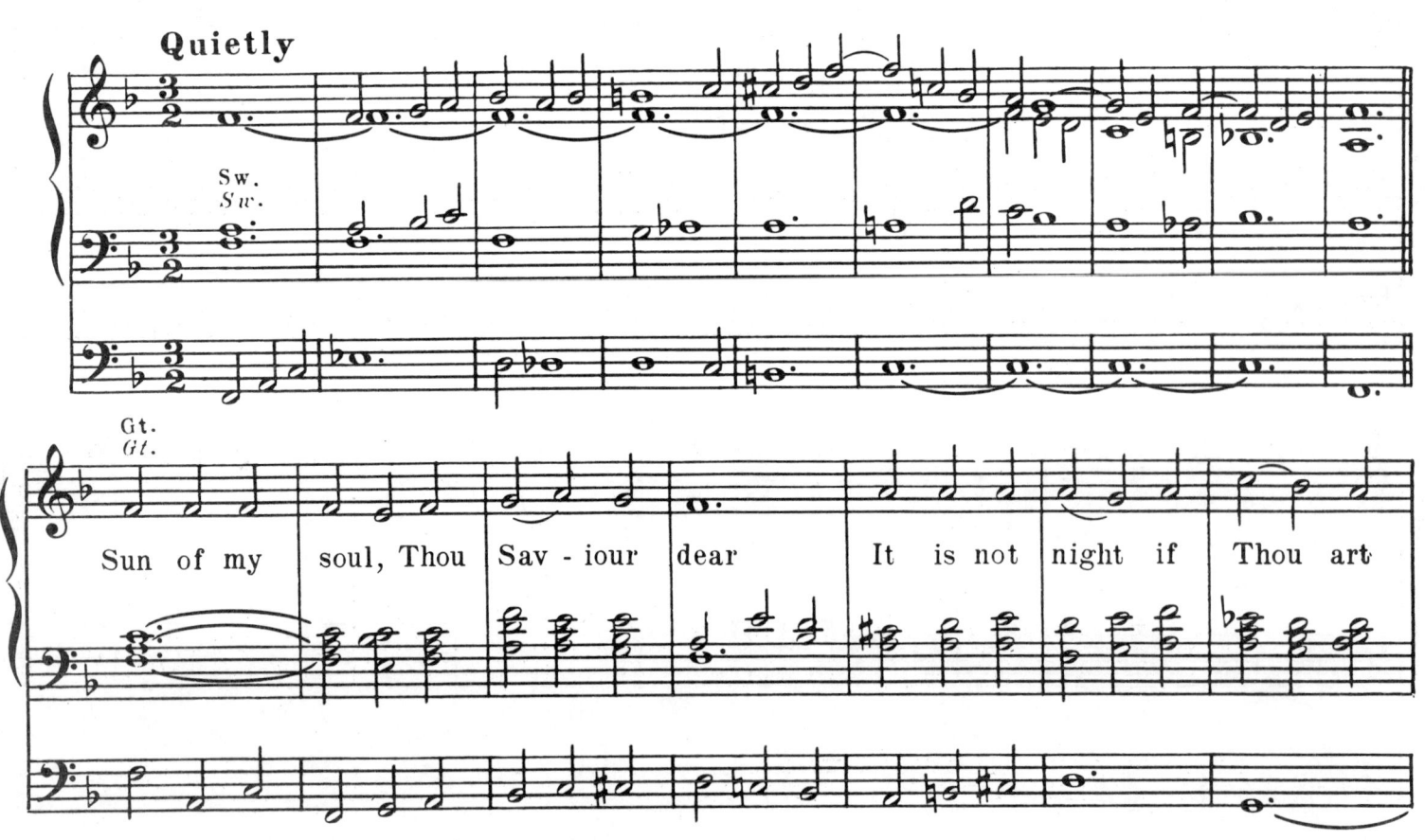

Copyright MCMXLVIII by Amsco Music Publishing Co., N.Y.C.

Made in U.S.A.

Communion Hymn
PICARDY

Registration 12

French Melody, 17th cent.

Christians Awake
CHRISTMAS HYMN

Registration 12

J. WAINRIGHT

Copyright MCMXLVIII by Amsco Music Publishing Co., N.Y.C.

Made in U.S.A.

Come, Sweet Peace

Registration 8

J. S. BACH

I Walked Into The Garden

Registration 10

MARION WEAVER

* Used by permission of Lewis Music Pub. Co., N.Y.C.

Made in U.S.A.

Open the Gates of the Temple

Registration 9

J. F. KNAPP

Onward Christian Soldiers

Registration 14

ARTHUR SULLIVAN

Mine Eyes Have Seen The Glory
(The Battle Hymn of the Republic)

Registration 15

J. W. HOWE - Wm. STEFFE

Copyright MCMXLVIII by Amsco Music Publishing Co., N.Y.C.

Made in U.S.A.

Luther's Cradle Hymn

Registration 9

Meditation
(Safe in the Arms of Jesus)

ROLAND DIGGLE

Star of the East
(CHRISTMAS SONG)

Registration 2

AMANDA KENNEDY

Copyright MCMXLVIII by Amsco Music Publishing Co., N.Y.C.

Made in U.S.A.

O Holy Night
(CHRISTMAS CAROL)

Registration 9

ADAM

Copyright MCMXLVIII by Amsco Music Publishing Co. N.Y.C.

Made in U.S.A.

It Came upon the Midnight Clear
(CHRISTMAS CAROL)

Registration 10

R. WILLIS

Copyright MCMXLVIII by Amsco Music Publishing Co., N.Y.C.

Made in U.S.A.

The First Noël

Registration 4

Traditional

Copyright MCMXLVIII by Amsco Music Publishing Co., N. Y. C.

Made in U. S. A.

154

O Come, All Ye Faithful

Registration 10

JOHN READING

Copyright MCMXLVIII by Amsco Music Publishing Co., N.Y.C.

Made in U.S.A.

Silent Night
(CHRISTMAS CAROL)
Arranged by Harry Vibbard

Registration 3

F. GRUBER

ALL ORGANS   PRE-SET MODELS   MODELS M & L 100

1.

Sw: 8' Strings
Gt: 8' Flute
    Sw. to Gt. 8' and 4'
Pedal: Soft 16', Sw. to Ped.

(A#) 00 4544 222

[A#] 00 5300 000

Pedal: 3-1
Vibrato: 2

M-100 SERIES
UPPER: 20 8585 530 LOWER: 8635 2210 PEDAL 4
M SERIES — VIBRATO: On, Normal
    PERCUSSION: Off

L-100 SERIES
UPPER: 20 8585 530 PEDAL 4
LOWER: 8635 221

2.

Sw: Celeste
    St. Diapason 8'
Gt: 8' Flute
    Sw. to Gt. 8' and 4'
Pedal: Soft 16'
    Sw. to Pedal

(A#) 00 5444 322

[A#] 00 5320 000

Pedal: 4-2

Vibrato: 2

M-100 SERIES
UPPER: 50 7738 536 LOWER: 8754 0542 PEDAL 4
M SERIES — VIBRATO: On, Normal
    PERCUSSION: Off

L-100 SERIES
UPPER: 50 7738 536 PEDAL 4
LOWER: 8754 054

3.

Sw: Soft 8', 4', Strings
Gt.: Dulciana 8', Flute 8'
    Sw. to Gt. 8' and 4'
Pedal: Soft 16
    Sw. to Gt.

(A#) 00 3444 433

[A#] 00 7432 000

Pedal: 3-1

Vibrato: 2

M-100 SERIES
UPPER: 40 1234 555 LOWER: 5300 0000 PEDAL 3
M SERIES — VIBRATO: On, Small
    PERCUSSION: Off

L-100 SERIES
UPPER: 40 1234 555 PEDAL 3
LOWER: 5300 000

4.

Sw. Soft 8' and 4' Strings
    and Flutes
Gt: Flute 8', Gamba 8', Sw. to Gt.
Pedal: Soft 16', Sw. to Pedal

(A#) 00 4544 222

[A#] 00 7554 321

Pedal: 3-1

Vibrato: 2

M-100 SERIES
UPPER: 00 5444 322 LOWER: 5320 0000 PEDAL 3
M SERIES — VIBRATO: On, Small
    PERCUSSION: Off

L-100 SERIES
UPPER: 00 5444 322 PEDAL 3
LOWER: 5320 000

ALL ORGANS   PRE-SET MODELS   MODELS M & L 100

5.

Sw: Soft 8' and 4' Strings
Gt: 8' Flute, Sw. to Gt. 8'
Pedal: Soft 16', Sw. to Pedal

(A#) 00 3533 332

[A#] 00 5320 000

Pedal: 3-1

Vibrato: 2

M-100 SERIES
UPPER: 31 1324 322   LOWER: 7432 0000   PEDAL 2
M SERIES — VIBRATO: On, Small
PERCUSSION: Off

L-100 SERIES
UPPER: 31 1324 322   PEDAL 2
LOWER: 7432 000

6.

Sw: 8' and soft 4' Solo Combinations
Gt: Dulciana 8'
Pedal: Soft 16', Gt. to Pedal

(A#) 00 5383 410

[A#] 00 3330 000

Pedal: 3-1

Vibrato: 2

M-100 SERIES
UPPER: 40 4544 222   LOWER: 7554 3210   PEDAL 2
M SERIES — VIBRATO: On, Small
PERCUSSION: Off

L-100 SERIES
UPPER: 40 4544 222   PEDAL 2
LOWER: 7554 321

7.

Sw: Celeste, 8' Strings, St. Diapason 8'
Gt: 8' Flute, Sw. to Gt.
Pedal: Soft 16', Sw. to Pedal

(A#) 00 5477 332

[A#] 00 3310 000

Pedal: 4-2

Vibrato: 2

M-100 SERIES
UPPER: 00 3533 332   LOWER: 5320 0000   PEDAL 2
M SERIES — VIBRATO: On, Small
PERCUSSION: Off

L-100 SERIES
UPPER: 00 3533 332   PEDAL 2
LOWER: 5320 000

8.

Sw: 8' and 4' Solo Comb.
Gt: Dulciana 8'
Pedal: Soft 16', Gt. to Pedal

(A#) 01 7675 321

[A#] 00 4432 000

Pedal: 4-2

Vibrato: 2

M-100 SERIES
UPPER: 40 3444 322   LOWER: 5310 0000   PEDAL 2
M SERIES — VIBRATO: On, Small
PERCUSSION: Off

L-100 SERIES
UPPER: 40 3444 322   PEDAL 2
LOWER: 5310 000

ALL ORGANS   PRE-SET MODELS   MODELS M & L 100

9.

Sw: 8' Strings, St. Diap. 8'
Gt: 8' Flute, Sw. to Gt. 8'
      and 4'
Pedal: Soft 16', Sw. to Pedal

  00 5632 212

  00 5320 000

Pedal: 4-2

Vibrato: 2

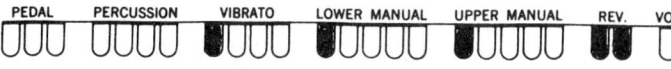
UPPER: 50 5477 332   LOWER: 5310 0000   PEDAL 3
M SERIES — VIBRATO: On, Small
PERCUSSION: Off

UPPER: 50 5477 332   PEDAL 3
LOWER: 5310 000

10.

Sw: 8' and 4' Strings, Flutes
      St. Diapason
Gt: To Gamba 8' and 4', Sw.
      to Gt.
Pedal: Soft 16' and 8', Sw. to
       Pedal

  00 7644 433

  00 4534 110

Pedal: 4-2

Vibrato: 2

UPPER: 01 7675 321   LOWER: 4432 0000   PEDAL 3
M SERIES — VIBRATO: On, Small
PERCUSSION: Off

UPPER: 01 7675 321   PEDAL 3
LOWER: 4432 000

11.

Sw: Celeste 8', St. Diap. 8'
Gt: 8' Flute, Sw. to Gt. 4'
Pedal: Soft 16', Sw. to Pedal

  00 2564 311

  00 8700 000

Pedal: 3-1

Vibrato: 2

UPPER: 00 5632 212   LOWER: 5320 0000   PEDAL 3
M SERIES — VIBRATO: On, Small
PERCUSSION: Off

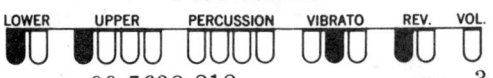
UPPER: 00 5632 212   PEDAL 3
LOWER: 5320 000

12.

Sw: 8' and 4' Strings, Flutes
Gt: Gamba 8', Flute 8', Sw. to
      Gt.
Pedal: Soft 16', Sw. to Pedal

  00 4533 322

  00 5641 100

Pedal: 4-2

Vibrato: 1

UPPER: 60 7644 321   LOWER: 4534 1100   PEDAL 3
M SERIES — VIBRATO: On, Small
PERCUSSION: Off

UPPER: 60 7644 321   PEDAL 3
LOWER: 4534 110

ALL ORGANS PRE-SET MODELS MODELS M & L 100

13.

Sw: Clarinet 8', Strings 8'
Gt: String Diapason 8'
Pedal: Soft 16', Sw. to Pedal

(A#) 12 4556 660

[A#] 00 6405 000

Pedal: 5-3

Vibrato: 2

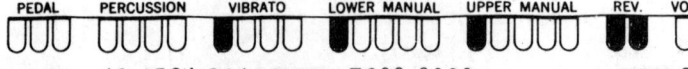
UPPER: 40 2564 311 LOWER: 7600 0000 PEDAL 2
M SERIES — VIBRATO: On, Small
PERCUSSION: Off

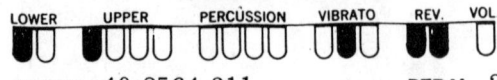
UPPER: 40 2564 311 PEDAL 2
LOWER: 7600 000

14.

Sw: Trombone 16'
    Trumpet 8'
Gt: String Diapason 8'
Pedal: Soft 16', Sw. to Pedal

(A#) 00 6784 662

[A#] 00 6653 422

Pedal: 4-2

Vibrato: 2

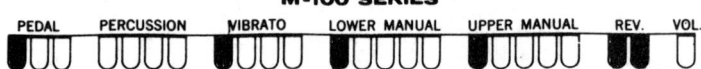
UPPER: 00 5443 211 LOWER: 5320 0000 PEDAL 2
M SERIES — VIBRATO: On, Small
PERCUSSION: Off

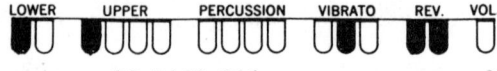
UPPER: 00 5443 211 PEDAL 2
LOWER: 5320 000

15.

Sw: Full Solo Combination
    (Strings 16', 8', 4',
    Reeds 8')
Gt: Open Diapason 8'
Pedal: Soft 16', Sw. to Pedal

(A#) 50 8655 314

[A#] 22 8833 455

Pedal: 4-2

Vibrato: 2

UPPER: 40 4533 322 LOWER: 5641 1000 PEDAL 3
M SERIES — VIBRATO: On, Small
PERCUSSION: Off

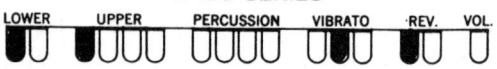
UPPER: 40 4533 322 PEDAL 3
LOWER: 5641 100